PRAISE FOR JT &
YOU ARE GREATNESS

"A common problem I used to struggle with was asking for help. Amazing things have always happened when I decided to put my faith in someone else I trust. That is where JT has been there for me over the years. He believed in me and helped change my mindset so that I was able to reach my greatness in life."

—Jordan Field

"Through the effective leading of JT, he has inspired me to be myself and to go after the things I truly want. Comfort in the past had me in PARK; now I'm in DRIVE and in full control of my steering wheel. Now the only thing I strive to be and look for is greatness.

The best decision of my life was saying YES to 'Thinking Into Results' since studying this I have attracted an abundance of opportunities. With JT's guidance, I was able to say 'YES' to the opportunities that were going to stretch my mind and get me out of my comfort zone and put me towards my goals.

I've attracted two job promotions in the last three months, got engaged to the love of my life, gained two streams of income, and on the verge of starting my own business. I can honestly say that none of this would have happened without the help of JT and 'Thinking Into Results.'"

—Travis Dezan

"JT has been a great source of encouraging and support since we met. The most significant achievement for me along this journey is to learn how to face the fear of scarcity and overcome it. I believe fear only can be replaced by courage, and even courage comes from inside. Courage is activated is by an external voice and JT has been that voice for me. 'You can do it Luis, you have it, you are greatness.' Thank you God for putting JT across my way."

—Luis Posse

"JT has helped me incredibly with seeing and believing the better things in life, and accepting them for what they are. He has mentored me to a better and more positive state of mind in order to achieve greatness in life, which I am forever grateful for."

—Kyle Donnelly

"As an entrepreneur and an individual who strives to become the best version of myself—I arrived at a point where hustling and reading books alone wasn't enough. I reached a plateau. I've hopped from one course or coaching program to another, with no results to show. At best, I would have a short period of growth before things went back to the way they were. Thinking Into Results and JT have become my unfair advantage at achieving my next level. The changes in my life through TIR have not only increased my income but also made me a better leader, boyfriend and friend. I've adopted new long-lasting habits and routines that resonates with my goals and the life I want."

—David Wong

"JT has found the environment where he can fly, so to speak, having discovered his potential to connect 'heart to heart' with those of us that are stuck or have lost our way. Conversations with JT have become uplifting and informative for me as I have benefited greatly from his teachings about the power of the subconscious mind. Reflecting on my own journey with him, his insight and enthusiasm disarm the self-doubters and the skeptics.

I taught for 30 years in English, Science, Physical Education, Special Education and eventually joined the guidance staff. I also coached seventy-five athletic teams where I shared with athletes the kinds of behaviour that would let them achieve their athletic and personal goals. I achieved moderate success but rarely took the risks necessary to grow from the inside out, a term I recently discovered through a self-help program offered through the Proctor-Gallagher Institute.

I finally took a chance in my second year of retirement from teaching and signed up for Bob Proctor's 'Thinking Into Results.' In a few short weeks, I experienced the many benefits the program had to offer about how our thoughts control our attitude and eventually the results we see in relationships, our jobs, and our more elaborate goals which Bob called 'fantasies.' Looking back on my 30 years as a high school educator, coach and counsellor, if I had known then what I know now, my students would have benefited from Bob's program tremendously. I also would have been stronger mentally and physically which would have gone a long way to sustaining my enthusiasm for my vocation.

I highly recommend that this program be embedded in the curriculum of both elementary and high school grades so as to complement the pursuit of academic excellence, athletic performance and overall well-being."

—**Brad McGhie,** *Physical Education and Guidance Teacher (30 years in education)*

"Since taking the Thinking Into Results program and working with JT as a coach, I have been inspired to live my life with more intention and in the present moment while preparing for future goals. I am able to take many of the concepts and implement them into the classroom to inspire students who struggle to make decisions, take responsibility and empower themselves to meet their goals as well as maximize their potential.

I highly recommend the Thinking Into Results program be implemented into education and work with JT who has training and expertise as well as an education background, to elevate educators and ensure each student is successful as a whole approach system: academically, emotionally and spiritually. These fundamentals for growth development are necessary parts and what every parent wants for their child. Collaboration with JT allows for this process to unfold and steer in a meaningful and fulfilling life."

—Gwen Steller, English, Student Success
and Resource Teacher (15 years in education)

"There are a thousand books out there that will teach you about greatness. In this book JT will not only teach you about greatness, but how to achieve it and find it in your life. Anyone can make a book for people to read, few can make a book that will change your approach to life and give you the tools to achieve greatness in your own life."

—Ben Koczwara, Pro Football Player

"Go alongside JT and follow his journey, personal growth, and change of mindset. Each chapter not only teaches you new lessons and tips, but challenges you to think of how you can apply them to your own life.

This book goes beyond stories and ideas. It is a workbook for you to plan and build a blueprint for your very own success!"

—**Nick Hallett**, *2019 Grey Cup Champion, Winnipeg Blue Bombers*

YOU ARE GREATNESS

VOLUME 1

13

IDEAS TO EFFORTLESSLY BRING JOY, CALM AND PEACE INTO YOUR LIFE

trazer alegria

JT TSUI

você é grandeza.

YOU ARE GREATNESS

13

IDEAS TO EFFORTLESSLY BRING JOY, CALM AND PEACE INTO YOUR LIFE

VOLUME 1

trazer alegria

JT TSUI

GLOBAL WELLNESS MEDIA
STRATEGIC EDGE INNOVATIONS PUBLISHING
LOS ANGELES, TORONTO, MONTRÉAL

For permission requests, send an email to Book@YouAreGreatnessBook.com

First Edition. Published by:
Global Wellness Media
Strategic Edge Innovations Publishing
340 S Lemon Ave #2027
Walnut, California 91789-2706
(866) 467-9090
StrategicEdgeInnovations.com

Publisher's Note: The views expressed in this work are solely those of the authors and do not necessarily reflect the views of the publisher, and the publisher hereby disclaims any responsibilities for them.

Book and Cover Design: Eric D. Groleau

You Are Greatness / JT Tsui. — 1st ed.
ISBN: 978-1-7363047-4-7 (Kindle)
ISBN: 978-1-7363047-5-4 (Paperback)

DISCLAIMER

The information contained herein is not intended to be a substitute for medical or financial advice. Counselling with professionals is always recommended.

This book is based on the author's personal experience and other real-life examples. To protect privacy, names may have been changed in some cases.

TABLE OF CONTENTS

prefacio

FOREWORD

I met JT a few years ago at a health and wellness product show hosted by my gym. I met many others that day too. However, JT stood out. *St disumentau* Why? I was immediately struck by JT's curiosity. He was completely fascinated with every conversation he had, including the one with me. I have long believed that being genuinely fascinated by learning will take you toward mastery of what it is you are passionate about. *lleval pora maestrix* Curiosity can give you the clarity of purpose that can facilitate your success—as you define it. JT truly lives a curious life — one that puts him the serve of others.

Leaving things to chance or circumstance does not even enter JT's mind. He passionately believes that life's *volante inta* steering wheel is firmly in his hands. This mindset brings great relief to oneself, and it releases one from the pressures of external forces that are not in our control. Justin carries this same message to his clients.

"If it's to be, it's up to me" is a strong message in JT's life and in this book. These are easy words to say, but it is not always easy to understand your path. JT's stepwise approach of helping you be curious enough to find your inner voice, and then your direction, is right on target. Justin's core message of 13 ideas for supporting a fulfilled life is fresh and thoughtful — anchored in a healthy focus on self and the capabilities that lie within.

Malcolm Eade, President and Chief Executive Officer,
Salus Global Corporation

ACKNOWLEDGEMENTS

I first want to acknowledge you for choosing to invest your time and energy into getting this book and helping me spread this message of GREATNESS.

Next, I want to thank my wife, Elesha, and my kids, Tyler and Kiyena, for unconditionally loving and supporting me during my growth journey. Your love, patience and compassion have inspired me to continually push myself to grow into the greatest version of myself.

I also wish to thank my mom, my two aunts and my grandfather for always believing in me and encouraging me to follow my heart and to trust my inner guidance.

Many thanks to my friend and publisher Eric D. Groleau, who not only designed the cover for this book, but was always ready to lend a helping hand, providing me with support whenever I needed it and helping me bring my vision of this book to life.

Words cannot express my gratitude to Danielle Amos for introducing Bob Proctor, his teachings and the *Thinking Into Results* program to our family. Your embodiment of this Bob's teaching has shown me what is possible for me as I have developed greater belief in myself. It has strengthened my relationship with Elesha and helped me develop a deeper connection to my kids, which is truly the greatest gift of all.

I also want to thank Doug Dane for his continued guidance and mentorship as he has helped me to let go of the things that were keeping me stuck and for showing me how to live with more love, joy and peace.

Lastly, I want to thank my good friend Malcolm Eade for writing the foreword for the book and for capturing the essence of the messages with such clarity and beauty.

With gratitude,

JT

DEDICATION

This book is dedicated to my beautiful wife, Elesha, and my two amazing kids, Tyler and Kiyena.

Thank you for always believing in me.

INTRODUCTION

On Mother's Day in 2016, I was rushed to the hospital with a suspected appendicitis,

I spent four days there hooked up to machines and in pain. This happened less than 24 hours before a highly anticipated job interview that I had been eagerly waiting to be available for a few years. As I lay in my hospital bed getting assessed by a team of doctors and going through a battery of tests, I experienced the greatest pain I had ever felt, both physically and emotionally.

It was in that hospital bed that I started to ask myself some difficult questions.

Am I living my best life?

What happens the next time I come to the hospital?

Am I prepared to leave my wife and young kids without a husband and father?

It was that four-day hospital visit where I started to fall in love with personal growth and self-development. Through the many years of my ongoing personal growth journey, I have learned so many important life lessons. In this short book, I want to share with you 13 ideas that helped me understand…

Eu sou grandeza

I AM GREATNESS

and

você é grandeza

YOU ARE GREATNESS

too!

This book has been written as a 'choose your own adventure.' Take time to read (and re-read) each story, reflect on the insight gained and apply it to your life moving forward.

As you begin to take focused and inspired action, you will continually improve the results in all areas of your life.

BONUS MATERIAL
& RESOURCES

Access printable exercise sheets and bonus
material, including my newest tool:

7 Questions to Get You Unstuck.

Visit:
https://youaregreatnessbook.com/bookbonus

Chapter 1

I AM AMBITIOUS

Porque se encaixar quando

> "Why fit in when you were
> born to stand out."

você nasceu para se destacar

—Dr. Seuss

**Would you like to achieve greatness?
To get the most, from this chapter try
the following exercise first:**

Repeat the following affirmations out
loud and with enthusiasm.

I AM AMBITIOUS

I AM AMBITIOUS

I AM AMBITIOUS

I AM AMBITIOUS

I AM AMBITIOUS

As long as I can remember, I have always been a curious individual. This curiosity gave me a tendency to always strive for more—to learn more about other people, to learn new things and to learn different ways to grow and better myself.

From a young age, I was conditioned to believe that curiosity was not a good character trait. I have early memories of a loved one who told me "You ask too many questions" and as I got older, friends who would ask, "So what are you into now?" These comments made me feel self-conscious for most of my life and I placed too much emphasis on what other people thought of me. As humans we have a deep desire to feel accepted, so I learned pretty quickly that the easy way to fit in, was to not stand out. During different times in history being accepted by others was literally the difference between life and death. If you were banished from the community as a caveman or cavewoman, your chances of survival were not good. The challenge is that always wanting to fit in is why most people feel stuck. They are playing the game of life based on other people's rules.

I want to share with you a different idea: your ambition is a superpower. Wanting more is part of who we naturally are—runners want to run faster and farther, people in sales want to sell more, trees want to grow taller, you get the point.

Where did I develop my ambition from? I have no doubt that I learned it from observing my mom at a young age. When I was seven years old, my mom completed her Masters in Business Administration (MBA). Despite her responsibilities as a wife, a primary caregiver to a young child, and a full-time career my mom went to school part-time at night and on weekends to complete her MBA. I still have vivid memories of sitting in a big lecture hall at York University playing as she was in class because she didn't have other childcare options. My mom's ambition to achieve more in her career, to earn more and to provide our family with a better life outweighed her desire to take it easy. What did this teach me? If you want something in life, you pull up your sleeves and go after it.

Now, do you really want to feel great?

Repeat the following affirmations out loud.
This time with more energy and enthusiasm.

I AM AMBITIOUS

I AM AMBITIOUS

I AM AMBITIOUS

I AM AMBITIOUS

I AM AMBITIOUS

Allow yourself to feel these words and do the following exercise to strengthen your mind-body connection.

**Complete the following exercise to achieve
GREATNESS in your life.**

You can download a printable exercise sheet on the bonus page (**https://youaregreatnessbook.com/bookbonus**) or use a piece of paper or journal for this. Don't do this on a phone or computer. There is something powerful about putting pen to paper and writing down.

3 P's EXERCISE

Purpose

Write your goal down (in the present tense).
Ex: "I am so happy and grateful now that..."

_____

_____

_____

_____

_____

_____

Plan

What was an insight you got from reading this chapter today?

_____

_____

_____

_____

_____

Principles

What actions will you apply to your life based on reading this chapter?

_____

_____

_____

_____

_____

Chapter 2

I AM BELIEF

*"Whether you think you can, or you
think you can't you're right."*

—Henry Ford

**To get the most, from this chapter try the
following exercise first:**

Repeat the following affirmations out loud
and with enthusiasm.

I AM BELIEF

I AM BELIEF

I AM BELIEF

I AM BELIEF

I AM BELIEF

I have been blessed to spend 35+ years in the sports world, first as
an athlete then as a coach working with athletes at many different
levels. One lesson I've learned from working with athletes at any
level of sport is this … the most successful ones have a strong belief
in themselves.

What is belief?

To me belief is having a deep understanding of how to best use your time, gifts, abilities and talents. When you maximize your time, gifts, abilities and talents you feel prepared for anything that life can throw at you. It's the ability to be calm and confident, regardless of what it says on the scoreboard of life at any moment.

During my last year of coaching high school football, our team made a commitment to make practice more intense than the game. The reason for this was that when you practice all week at the highest level possible then things seem to slow down on game day. When things slow down on game day, that gives you the ability to play fast—when you play fast great things always happen.

Our goal from the start of our off-season program was to "BRING IT HOME" which meant we wanted to win our league championship. The league championship was named after one of our assistant coaches' dad who also happened to be my position coach in university—it had a special meaning to all of us. At the start of every practice one of our coaches led our players through our "BRING IT HOME" program on the field. The program consisted of 4–5 minutes of physical conditioning which not only pushed the limits of our player's physical bodies; it also pushed their mental capacities. As our team progressed through the "BRING IT HOME" program their physical and mental conditioning improved and their belief strengthened. When things got tough in games our players had developed such a deep belief in themselves, their teammates and our coaches that they always found ways to make and create plays.

Guess what?

We did "BRING IT HOME" that year!

Whether on the field of sport or the game of life, when you develop a strong belief in yourself you understand that you always have the ability to make a play. When you realize that you have this power there is no challenge or obstacle that you cannot overcome.

Repeat the following affirmations out loud.
This time with more energy and enthusiasm.

I AM BELIEF

I AM BELIEF

I AM BELIEF

I AM BELIEF

I AM BELIEF

Allow yourself to feel these words and do the following exercise to strengthen your mind-body connection. Grab your piece of paper or journal again.

3 P's EXERCISE

Purpose

Write your goal down (in the present tense).
Ex: "I am so happy and grateful now that..."

_____

_____

_____

_____

_____

_____

Plan

What was an insight you got from reading this chapter today?

_____

_____

_____

_____

_____

_____

Principles

What actions will you apply to your life based on reading this chapter?

_____

_____

_____

_____

_____

Chapter 3

I AM CONSISTENT

"Success is the progressive realization
of a worthy goal or ideal."

—Earl Nightingale

**To get the most, from this chapter try the
following exercise first:**

Repeat the following affirmations out loud
and with enthusiasm.

I AM CONSISTENT

I AM CONSISTENT

I AM CONSISTENT

I AM CONSISTENT

I AM CONSISTENT

One of the greatest lessons I learned from my mentor, Bob Proctor, is that success in life is very simple—it's 95% mindset and 5% strategy. To create better results in any area of your life you must first focus on creating more effective and focused habits. Why are habits so powerful? 96–98% of the time we are operating on our habits—everything you think about, everything you say, your perspective of the world and most importantly what you do is habitual.

The one habit that transformed my life is when I started to invest more time and energy into my most valuable resource, ME. To make sure I prioritized this daily investment of time and energy I scheduled it first thing in my morning so I made sure that it got done. I found the more energy I poured into myself the more I had to give others, which is what I love to do.

As with any change everything starts when you make a committed decision to take action. At first, I started to wake up earlier, move my body and listen to personal growth podcasts. Then I started to meditate after my workout. I started to feel better because I had more energy and focus so I wanted to start tweaking my habits even more. I started looking for new and better ways to improve all areas of my life—my health, my relationships, my finances, my career and my life. Then I came to one big aha—that creating better results in any area of life started when I changed my mindset. I found ways to get more comfortable being uncomfortable every day, the more discomfort, the bigger the growth and the better the results.

As I got more consistent investing time and energy into myself, the results in all areas of my life changed for the better. As the results changed a funny thing happened, I actually spent *less* time doing and *more* time being present AND my results have continually gotten better.

What area of your life would you like to achieve better results in?

Health? Relationships? Finances? Work/Career? Lifestyle?

What specific action will you commit to taking for the next two weeks to improve your results?

Remember all change starts with one new action.

> Repeat the following affirmations out loud.
> This time with more energy and enthusiasm.
>
> **I AM CONSISTENT**
>
> **I AM CONSISTENT**
>
> **I AM CONSISTENT**
>
> **I AM CONSISTENT**
>
> **I AM CONSISTENT**

Allow yourself to feel these words and do the following exercise to strengthen your mind-body connection. Grab your piece of paper or journal again.

3 P's EXERCISE

Purpose

Write your goal down (in the present tense).

Ex: "I am so happy and grateful now that..."

Plan

What was an insight you got from reading this chapter today?

Principles

What actions will you apply to your life based on reading this chapter?

Chapter 4

I AM DECISIVE

"Successful people make decisions quickly and firmly. Unsuccessful people make decisions slowly, and they change them often."

—Napoleon Hill

To get the most, from this chapter try the following exercise first:

Repeat the following affirmations out loud and with enthusiasm.

I AM DECISIVE

I AM DECISIVE

I AM DECISIVE

I AM DECISIVE

I AM DECISIVE

One fall afternoon in 2019 I met a friend for coffee and we ended up spending some time chatting about life. During our conversation, he asked me, "Have you ever thought about running an extreme race?" The interesting thing is I had thought about running a race off and on for years but never entertained the idea past that. On the way home on the GO Train that day, I made the committed decision that I was going to enter and run the Scotiabank Toronto Waterfront Half-Marathon. As soon as I got home, I went onto my computer and officially registered for the race, which by the way was only 37 days away. As soon as I registered for this half-marathon (it's a 21 km race), some of my old limiting beliefs started to come up in my head—who are you to do this as you have never even attempted to run a 5 km or 10 km race, you have not run in close to four months so you won't be ready in 37 days, you shouldn't run as you're still recovering from a pretty significant case of adrenal fatigue (aka "burnout").

I decided that I had two goals for my upcoming race. First, I wanted to run the half-marathon in less than two hours and 10 minutes. Second, I wanted to run the entire race without any walking. I did my best to prepare over the next five and a half weeks, training for the race went well, especially for a first timer.

On the day of the race I felt strong, powerful and was running well. I was flooded with the same feelings and emotions that I used to experience on game day as a football player and coach. I had been really craving these feelings of exhilaration and purpose in my life and I had found it. Then everything changed as I passed the 16 km marker of the race. As soon as I passed the marker, I started to experience significant pain in both my knees, my upper thighs started to tighten but more importantly my mind started to play tricks on me. All of a sudden I started to hear this inner voice telling me "If it hurts, just start walking," "There is no harm in quitting" and "You won't finish." It was in this moment when I realized I had two choices—stop running or focus on running one step at a time. I reminded myself what my goal in this race was—to finish in less than two hours and 10 minutes and run the whole race. I reminded myself the only way to accomplish my goal was to keep running, to focus on putting one foot in front of the other and breaking the race down into one kilometre intervals for smaller victories.

An amazing thing happened as soon as I made the committed decision that I was going to run, all of the physical and mental discomfort faded away. I realized in that moment that "I've got this" and I was flooded with emotions because I knew that I didn't allow the fear to stop from doing something I wanted.

I finished the run sprinting through the finish line in under two hours, 1 hour, 59 minutes and 57 seconds to be exact. The sense of accomplishment as I crossed that finish line was as great as any win I had experienced to date.

Repeat the following affirmations out loud. This time with more energy and enthusiasm.

I AM DECISIVE

I AM DECISIVE

I AM DECISIVE

I AM DECISIVE

I AM DECISIVE

Allow yourself to feel these words and do the following exercise to strengthen your mind-body connection. Grab your piece of paper or journal again.

3 P's EXERCISE

Purpose

Write your goal down (in the present tense).

Ex: "I am so happy and grateful now that..."

_____

_____

_____

_____

_____

_____

Plan

What was an insight you got from reading this chapter today?

_____

_____

_____

_____

_____

_____

Principles

What actions will you apply to your life based on reading this chapter?

_____

_____

_____

_____

_____

_____

Chapter 5

I AM ENERGETIC

*"Everything is energy and that's all there is to it.
Match the frequency of the reality you want and you
cannot help but get that reality. It can be no other
way. This is not philosophy. This is physics."*

—Albert Einstein

**To get the most, from this chapter try the
following exercise first:**

Repeat the following affirmations out loud
and with enthusiasm.

I AM ENERGETIC

I AM ENERGETIC

I AM ENERGETIC

I AM ENERGETIC

I AM ENERGETIC

As a former educator one of my favourite activities to do with all
my students and athletes were to give them leadership
opportunities. It didn't matter whether it was a grade 9 Physical

Education class, a grade 11 Fitness class, a grade 12 Recreational Leadership class or a Senior Football team I always wanted to find ways to develop and empower people as leaders.

Why is leadership important?

Being a good leader is a life skill that will allow you to thrive in any environment.

One of the first things I did at the start of every semester or season was to find ways to model effective leadership early and often. I would ask for volunteers to lead a warm-up, I would ask for people to help me demonstrate drills/games and I would even have formal assignments for my senior classes to help lead the younger grades. All of this was simply practice to get better and refine their leadership skills—to improve any skill it's a matter of focused reps and sets.

I believe that all effective leaders do one thing very well—they 'Bring IT.'

What is "IT"?

IT is your best energy and your best attitude.

A good leader understands that by bringing their best energy and attitude is how they can be of service to others. It's about helping others achieve what they want by putting them in a position to succeed and thrive.

No, it's not about faking it to make it because that is a big load of BS.

You "Bring IT" by putting all of your energy into giving others the best experience and leaving them better than before you got there.

Repeat the following affirmations out loud.
This time with more energy and enthusiasm.

I AM ENERGETIC

I AM ENERGETIC

I AM ENERGETIC

I AM ENERGETIC

I AM ENERGETIC

Allow yourself to feel these words and do the following exercise to strengthen your mind-body connection. Grab your piece of paper or journal again.

3 P's EXERCISE

Purpose

Write your goal down (in the present tense).
Ex: "I am so happy and grateful now that..."

_____

_____

_____

_____

_____

_____

Plan

What was an insight you got from reading this chapter today?

_____

_____

_____

_____

_____

_____

Principles

What actions will you apply to your life based on reading this chapter?

_____

_____

_____

_____

_____

_____

Chapter 6

I AM FAITH

"Take pride in how far you've come.
Have faith in how far you can go. But
don't forget to enjoy the journey."

—Michael Josephson

To get the most, from this chapter try the
following exercise first:

Repeat the following affirmations out loud
and with enthusiasm.

I AM FAITH

I AM FAITH

I AM FAITH

I AM FAITH

I AM FAITH

Growing up, I had a complicated relationship with the idea of faith. From a young age, my mom and grandparents would bring me to church every weekend but it never resonated with me. As a teenager I would volunteer to drive my grandparents to church on the weekends and I would drop them off and tell them I was sitting by myself. Little did they know that I was really walking to go get a slice of pizza and a drink every weekend. It wasn't until my late 30s that I started to accept a new idea of what faith actually meant.

For most of my life, I thought that faith was your religious beliefs but as I became more open-minded my view changed. Today, I believe that faith is simply understanding that there is a higher power beyond you—it could be God, Source, Infinite Intelligence, Allah, Universe, etc.

This belief has transformed my life because I now finally understand that everything in life is always happening FOR ME.

Are there moments when I feel frustrated, worried or angry?

Absolutely.

I chose not to sit in those emotions and feelings for very long because they won't help me live a great life. As one of my mentors taught me, allow your emotions to run to and through you. I understand that in every situation in life there are always opportunities to learn and grow.

Repeat the following affirmations out loud.
This time with more energy and enthusiasm.

I AM FAITH

I AM FAITH

I AM FAITH

I AM FAITH

I AM FAITH

Allow yourself to feel these words and do the following exercise to strengthen your mind-body connection. Grab your piece of paper or journal again.

3 P's EXERCISE

Purpose

Write your goal down (in the present tense).

Ex: "I am so happy and grateful now that..."

_____

_____

_____

_____

_____

Plan

What was an insight you got from reading this chapter today?

_____

_____

_____

_____

_____

Principles

What actions will you apply to your life based on reading this chapter?

_____

_____

_____

_____

_____

Chapter 7

I AM GRATEFUL

"Gratitude and not expressing it is like
wrapping a present and not giving it."

—William Arthur Ward

**To get the most, from this chapter try the
following exercise first:**

Repeat the following affirmations out loud
and with enthusiasm.

I AM GRATEFUL

I AM GRATEFUL

I AM GRATEFUL

I AM GRATEFUL

I AM GRATEFUL

After a health scare in 2016, I started to ask different questions like "what am I doing with my life?" This prompted me to start reading books and listening to podcasts regarding personal growth and self-development. I fell in love with the ideas I was reading about and listening to and started to make different choices in my life.

These choices impacted every area of my life from my health—starting to move my body every morning before work, my spirituality—I started to meditate every day, my wealth—the things I started to spend and invest my money into, and my purpose—what I wanted to do with my life. Essentially it made me more aware of who I am and what I want my life to look like.

In this process I started a daily gratitude practice in which I would write down 5–10 things that I was grateful for every morning.

Why did I start this gratitude practice?

I had read and heard from many other successful and highly effective people that a daily gratitude practice was a non-negotiable for them. For most of my life, I had been an unhappy and negative person away from teaching and coaching.

I finally understood why a daily gratitude practice was so powerful on September 27, 2019. As I was walking home from my outdoor workout on a warm beautiful fall day with sunny blue skies, I realized something. This was the day that the sale of our old house was closing, we had already moved the month prior. I was immediately flooded with a deep sense of gratitude for my life, there was this calm, peace, and ease that I really had not experienced a lot prior to this moment.

I was in the process of pursuing a new adventure in my life, striving for a different way of living and going against societal norms. By mainstream standards I was losing, I had resigned from a guaranteed six-figure income job that I was very good at, I was no longer a homeowner, I had a "side business" that was not consistently bringing in any money, and I just sold my car. The truth was I never felt more grateful, at peace and free. I let go of the fear that I had allowed to hold me back for many years and I decided to start living with more FAITH in myself and this journey I felt called to pursue.

Repeat the following affirmations out loud.
This time with more energy and enthusiasm.

I AM GRATEFUL

I AM GRATEFUL

I AM GRATEFUL

I AM GRATEFUL

I AM GRATEFUL

Allow yourself to feel these words and do the following exercise to strengthen your mind-body connection. Grab your piece of paper or journal again.

3 P's EXERCISE

Purpose

Write your goal down (in the present tense).

Ex: "I am so happy and grateful now that..."

_____

_____

_____

_____

_____

_____

Plan

What was an insight you got from reading this chapter today?

_____

_____

_____

_____

_____

_____

Principles

What actions will you apply to your life based on reading this chapter?

_____

_____

_____

_____

_____

_____

Chapter 8

I AM HONEST

*"We can never obtain peace in the
outer world until we make
peace with ourselves."*

—Buddha

**To get the most, from this chapter try the
following exercise first:**

Repeat the following affirmations out loud
and with enthusiasm.

I AM HONEST

I AM HONEST

I AM HONEST

I AM HONEST

I AM HONEST

One of the most humbling experiences for me was leaving a successful 15-year career as a high school educator. For many years of my life teaching was the one area that I always felt calm and confident because it always made sense to me. When I walked away from the safe and comfortable world of teaching, I felt lost and confused because I removed the one thing that felt easy to me, my self-confidence was at an all-time low.

Becoming an entrepreneur and starting my own business has been an "interesting" process, to say the least. It has forced me to confront all my doubts, worries, insecurities and fears—some that I didn't even know existed. I realized that many of my doubts, worries and fears about entrepreneurship, business, sales, etc. came from watching many of the struggles and challenges that I observed my parents go through growing up, especially my dad.

Yes, my parents did the best they could and they provided me with everything I could ever want. But I quickly realized for me to achieve what I wanted in my life I had to learn from my past and take full responsibility for my results moving forward.

How did I do this?

I had to get honest with myself and learn this one fundamental truth.

I AM GREATNESS.

I want you to know YOU ARE GREATNESS too.

Learning and understanding this truth has been a life-transforming idea because it reminds me how much potential is inside of me. What keeps me stuck, at times, is that I sometimes forget my truth "I AM GREATNESS." When you understand and apply this truth to any area of your life, greatness will ensue.

It's amazing how when you connect to your truth that **I AM GREATNESS** that all the doubt, worry, insecurities and fear start to fade away. When this happens, you start to take focused action and when you take focused action this is how more success starts to roll into your life.

Repeat the following affirmations out loud.
This time with more energy and enthusiasm.

I AM HONEST

I AM HONEST

I AM HONEST

I AM HONEST

I AM HONEST

Allow yourself to feel these words and do the following exercise to strengthen your mind-body connection. Grab your piece of paper or journal again.

3 P's EXERCISE

Purpose

Write your goal down (in the present tense).

Ex: "I am so happy and grateful now that..."

_____

_____

_____

_____

_____

_____

Plan

What was an insight you got from reading this chapter today?

_____

_____

_____

_____

_____

_____

Principles

What actions will you apply to your life based on reading this chapter?

_____

_____

_____

_____

_____

_____

Chapter 9

I AM ILLOGICAL

*"A journey of a thousand miles
begins with one step."*

—Lao Tzu

**To get the most, from this chapter try the
following exercise first:**

Repeat the following affirmations out loud
and with enthusiasm.

I AM ILLOGICAL

I AM ILLOGICAL

I AM ILLOGICAL

I AM ILLOGICAL

I AM ILLOGICAL

The last six months of my teaching career were very challenging because I felt stuck and it impacted every area of my life. I felt so stuck that I had to take a one-week leave of absence in February, then a three-week leave of absence in June and many "sick days" in between.

That is the interesting thing with logic: it keeps you right where you are. For me I knew I did not want to be living the life I was at the time but I was being indecisive and delaying the decision that I wanted to make. The decision I wanted to make was to pursue a new adventure in life—to invest more time with my family, to help more people and to travel to different parts of the world.

At the time, logic was telling me to stay in my teaching career, to stay living in London (Ontario), to stay coaching football, etc. The problem was that this logic was based on other people's ideas of what it meant to live a great life.

Doing the illogical means you have to be willing to make a decision and do things that make you uncomfortable each and every day. The more uncomfortable it makes you feel the better because it means it is challenging you to grow. The more you grow, the more your awareness changes, the more your awareness changes the better your results.

Writing this book was even illogical as I came up with the idea on a run. I made the decision that I wanted to write a book, I was going to do it in two weeks and this is what I was going to talk about.

> Repeat the following affirmations out loud.
> This time with more energy and enthusiasm.
>
> **I AM ILLOGICAL**
>
> **I AM ILLOGICAL**
>
> **I AM ILLOGICAL**
>
> **I AM ILLOGICAL**
>
> **I AM ILLOGICAL**

Allow yourself to feel these words and do the following exercise to strengthen your mind-body connection. Grab your piece of paper or journal again.

3 P's EXERCISE

Purpose

Write your goal down (in the present tense).
Ex: "I am so happy and grateful now that..."

_____

_____

_____

_____

_____

_____

Plan

What was an insight you got from reading this chapter today?

_____

_____

_____

_____

_____

_____

Principles

What actions will you apply to your life based on reading this chapter?

_____

_____

_____

_____

_____

_____

Chapter 10

I AM JOY

*"The past has no power over
the present moment."*

—Eckhart Tolle

**To get the most, from this chapter try the
following exercise first:**

Repeat the following affirmations out loud
and with enthusiasm.

I AM JOY

I AM JOY

I AM JOY

I AM JOY

I AM JOY

I am so happy and grateful for my wife, Elesha, because she has always unconditionally loved and supported me. To this day I am still amazed that she stuck by me through all these years because I was often an unhappy, controlling and critical a#$%$#%.

Elesha's persistence of never giving up on me and always believing in me is why I am still here today.

One of the greatest lessons I have learned from Elesha is how to BE more present in my life. Learning to do this has taken a lot of conscious effort on my part but it has helped me experience a greater sense of joy and calm in my daily life.

One of the biggest lies I was conditioned to believe is the myth of "someday." I used to say things like...

"I'll be happy when I get that next promotion at work."

"I'll be happy when we pay off the mortgage."

"I'll be happy when we go on that next vacation."

"I'll be happy when I have this amount of money in my bank account."

"I'll be happy when..."

What I have learned is that when you say, "I'll be happy when...", what you are doing is delaying your happiness. You are training your mind to say that your happiness is tied to something outside of you (e.g. a car, a home, a vacation, money...) This will always lead you to feel unfulfilled and unsatisfied because you're constantly chasing the next shiny object.

It is more enjoyable to live every day in joy. For me, joy is learning to appreciate the simple moments of life—it is that morning cup of coffee, it is watching my kids laughing and playing together, it is the family pizza/sushi nights. Yes, our family likes to combine pizza and sushi together because that is what brings us joy.

What do you love to do?

What activities bring you joy?

What people bring you joy?

How can you bring more joy to your life?

Finding ways to bring yourself more joy is what makes life worth living.

Repeat the following affirmations out loud.
This time with more energy and enthusiasm.

I AM JOY

I AM JOY

I AM JOY

I AM JOY

I AM JOY

Allow yourself to feel these words and do the following exercise to strengthen your mind-body connection. Grab your piece of paper or journal again.

3 P's EXERCISE

Purpose

Write your goal down (in the present tense).

Ex: "I am so happy and grateful now that..."

_____
_____
_____
_____
_____

Plan

What was an insight you got from reading this chapter today?

_____
_____
_____
_____
_____

Principles

What actions will you apply to your life based on reading this chapter?

_____
_____
_____
_____
_____

Chapter 11

I AM KIND

*"If we all do one random act of kindness
daily, we just might set the world in
the right direction."*

—Martin Kornfield

**To get the most, from this chapter try the
following exercise first:**

Repeat the following affirmations out loud
and with enthusiasm.

I AM KIND

I AM KIND

I AM KIND

I AM KIND

I AM KIND

One of the biggest lessons I've learned over the last year is that you can't give to others what you don't already have yourself.

If you want to love others must first love yourself.

If you want to be calm to others, you must first be calm yourself.

If you want to be kind to others, you must first be kind to yourself.

In the process of making some big changes both personally and professionally I have been forced to confront some old-limiting beliefs. The "interesting" thing about these old limiting beliefs is that they aren't even yours and they are based on someone else's ideas. But make no mistake about the power of the old limiting beliefs they are powerful and the reason why most people stay and feel stuck.

Leaving my high school teaching career has helped me realize how much I allowed my identity was tied to my previous career. This process has really forced me to discover who I am but this has allowed me to connect to my unique gifts, talents and abilities. One of the lessons I've learned is that a "rich" life is achieved by focusing on enriching the lives of others.

Has the growth process been easy?

Absolutely not, but it has been so worth it.

Most of the time I have felt energized and enthused because I am learning more about myself, to be kinder to myself and this is allowing me to serve more people. On the other hand, it has made me feel very uncomfortable at times because I have become more aware of all my doubts, worries, insecurities and fears. To create change in any area of your life you must be willing to remove and release your doubts, worries, insecurities, and fears and start to replace them with joy, calm, confidence and ease.

Repeat the following affirmations out loud.
This time with more energy and enthusiasm.

I AM KIND

I AM KIND

I AM KIND

I AM KIND

I AM KIND

Allow yourself to feel these words and do the following exercise to strengthen your mind-body connection. Grab your piece of paper or journal again.

3 P's EXERCISE

Purpose

Write your goal down (in the present tense).

Ex: "I am so happy and grateful now that..."

_____

_____

_____

_____

_____

_____

Plan

What was an insight you got from reading this chapter today?

_____

_____

_____

_____

_____

_____

Principles

What actions will you apply to your life based on reading this chapter?

_____

_____

_____

_____

_____

_____

Chapter 12

I AM LOVE

"Darkness cannot drive over darkness; only light can do that. Hate cannot drive out hate; only love can do that."

—Dr. Martin Luther King Jr

To get the most, from this chapter try the following exercise first:

Repeat the following affirmations out loud and with enthusiasm.

I AM LOVE

I AM LOVE

I AM LOVE

I AM LOVE

I AM LOVE

I had an "interesting" relationship with my dad growing up. I remember him taking me to a Toronto Maple Leafs' game at the old Maple Leaf Gardens at the corner of Carlton Street and Church Street when I was six years old. I still remember that Toronto lost to the

Chicago Blackhawks 3-1 that night but I did get a wooden mini-stick with a foam puck that I loved. I have so many memories playing with the mini-stick and puck and creating my own epic solo hockey games.

I also remember waking up early on Sunday mornings to go with my dad to his military collectibles shows that he loved. After about the age of 9–10 my relationship with my father got more complicated and combative.

My memories after that are of a controlling, critical and angry man that was not very enjoyable to be around. Without a doubt I know deep down that my dad cared about me. He would drive two hours one way from Toronto to London (Ontario) to help me fix my car, he would take my family out for a meal and would give me his last dollar.

But all I truly wanted for him was to feel as if I was seen and heard. For many years I carried around a lot of resentment, bitterness and anger for how I felt my dad had treated me. The irony is for the first few years of my son's life I was often treating him in the same way that my dad had done with me—I was too controlling, too critical and too angry.

I came to the realization that for me to show up better for my son I needed to learn how to love myself first. I had to understand that fundamental truth that "I AM GREATNESS." As I have learned this simple and fundamental truth that every area of my life has improved.

In every moment you have the opportunity to make a new choice.

I accept the fact that my father did the best he could, based on his awareness.

I accept the fact that, in my past, I did the best I could, based on my level of awareness.

I accept the fact that my past decisions don't have to determine my future actions.

I accept that I'm teaching my son the fundamental truth that "I AM GREATNESS."

It's amazing how my relationship with my son has improved as I have worked on loving myself and modelling on how he can do the same.

Repeat the following affirmations out loud.
This time with more energy and enthusiasm.

I AM LOVE

I AM LOVE

I AM LOVE

I AM LOVE

I AM LOVE

Allow yourself to feel these words and do the following exercise to strengthen your mind-body connection. Grab your piece of paper or journal again.

3 P's EXERCISE

Purpose

Write your goal down (in the present tense).

Ex: "I am so happy and grateful now that..."

_____
_____
_____
_____
_____
_____

Plan

What was an insight you got from reading this chapter today?

_____
_____
_____
_____
_____
_____

Principles

What actions will you apply to your life based on reading this chapter?

_____
_____
_____
_____
_____
_____

Chapter 13

I AM MOMENTUM

"Imperfect action is better
than perfect inaction."

—Harry S. Truman

To get the most, from this chapter try the
following exercise first:

Repeat the following affirmations out loud
and with enthusiasm.

I AM MOMENTUM

I AM MOMENTUM

I AM MOMENTUM

I AM MOMENTUM

I AM MOMENTUM

I have been blessed to spend the last 35+ years involved in sport—first as an athlete and then as a coach. One of the most popular and commonly used words in sport is "momentum."

What is momentum?

Momentum is a state of mind.

It is a feeling.

When you feel great, you play great.

In sport as well as life, most people allow their current results (aka—the scoreboard) to control how they feel about their chances of success. Your current results are based on your past thoughts and actions—it's an indication where you are at this moment. Those that win in sport and life have developed the ability to observe their results neutrally—there is no meaning to them. Being able to observe other people and events in a neutral mindset is a core principle of any mindfulness-based training program.

How do you start to develop a neutral mind?

You must begin to train your mind to be still for a period of time every day.

When I started a new teaching job in 2016 after my health scare, I decided to start waking up early and moving my body before work. After a few weeks, I made the decision to download an app and start integrating a three-minute guided mindfulness activity after every morning workout. Initially I would fall asleep most mornings during my guided mindfulness activities which I later learned was part of the body's way of catching up on much-needed rest. I learned this when I invested into myself and attended a Vedic Meditation with one of my teachers and mentors.

This did take some conscious effort on my part to train my mind to be still but it has been one of the best gifts I've ever received. As I practice this daily, it became easier to be still and this taught me how to become more responsive and less reactive in my life. The ability to become more responsive has taught me how to stay in control regardless of what is happening outside of and around me.

Repeat the following affirmations out loud.
This time with more energy and enthusiasm.

I AM MOMENTUM

I AM MOMENTUM

I AM MOMENTUM

I AM MOMENTUM

I AM MOMENTUM

Allow yourself to feel these words and do the following exercise to strengthen your mind-body connection. Grab your piece of paper or journal again.

3 P's EXERCISE

Purpose

Write your goal down (in the present tense).

Ex: "I am so happy and grateful now that..."

_____

_____

_____

_____

_____

_____

Plan

What was an insight you got from reading this chapter today?

_____

_____

_____

_____

_____

_____

Principles

What actions will you apply to your life based on reading this chapter?

_____

_____

_____

_____

_____

_____

CONCLUSION

I am so happy and grateful that you have invested your time and energy into reading this book. One of the things I tell my clients is the greatest investment you can ever make is in yourself.

Why?

YOU ARE GREATNESS!

YOU DESERVE TO LOOK AND FEEL GREAT.

YOU DESERVE TO HAVE LOVING AND SUPPORTIVE RELATIONSHIPS.

YOU DESERVE TO EARN THE INCOME YOU WANT.

YOU DESERVE TO TREAT YOURSELF TO THE THINGS YOU LOVE

YOU DESERVE TO SPEND YOUR DAYS DOING WHAT YOU LOVE.

YOU ARE GREATNESS!

RESOURCES

SUGGESTED BOOKS

The following is a list of books I keep recommending to my clients.

- ***Think and Grow Rich*** by Napoleon Hill *(make sure you get this exact version "Classic Version.")*
  https://youaregreatnessbook.com/thinkandgrowrich
- ***You 2: A High Velocity Formula for Multiplying Your Personal Effectiveness in Quantum Leaps***, Price Pritchett
  https://youaregreatnessbook.com/you2

SUGGESTED MEDITATION

Meditation, calmness and relaxation are truly hidden jewels of success. When you master them, you'll find an unwavering confidence that draws your dreams and goals closer with each breath. For a more productive, enjoyable and relaxed life, I use and recommend a free meditation by mentor Bob Proctor. Bob has been at the forefront of the personal development industry for the last 60 years, he's a star of the hit movie The Secret and the best-selling author *You Were Born Rich*.

- ***Health + Wealth POWER Meditation***, by Bob Proctor
  https://youaregreatnessbook.com/powermeditation

ABOUT THE AUTHOR

 **JT Tsui** is a driven, passionate and service-oriented Coaching Professional with over 20+ years of leadership and management experience in athletics, education and business. JT consistently delivers strong results for his clients by creating equitable, diverse and inclusive environments where all team members can be in a position to reach their potential and succeed.

Prior to his current work, JT had a successful 15-year career as a High School Teacher working alongside students in Health & Physical Education and Student Success. Outside of the classroom JT has always believed in the importance of serving others and has spent the last 20 years coaching athletes at the local, high school, provincial and professional level in football, track & field, and hockey. To round off his experience, JT has also developed a diverse background of leadership experiences at the community, school, and school board level.

For more information about JT and to connect with him, visit:

JTTSUI.com

NOTES

NOTES

NOTES

NOTES

NOTES

NOTES

BONUS MATERIAL
& RESOURCES

Access printable exercise sheets and bonus
material, including my newest tool:

7 Questions to Get You Unstuck.

Visit:
https://youaregreatnessbook.com/bookbonus